Animal Farm A to Z:
A Coloring and Storybook Adventure

By

Yemi Oluwoye

1

Acknowledgment

With deep gratitude, I thank my family for their constant love and support. To my children and all the wonderful kids, I've had the joy of working with you are my greatest inspiration. To the educators who share this mission, thank you. And to every young reader: may this book spark your imagination and a lifelong love for learning.

A - Alpaca's Fluffy Adventure

On a bright morning at Happy Hoof Farm, Annie the Alpaca woke up feeling extra fluffy! She trotted to the barn, where Farmer Joe was brushing the sheep.
"Baa! You're the fluffiest animal on the farm!" said Sally the Sheep. Annie giggled. "I bet I can make the softest blanket with my wool!"
Farmer Joe sheared Annie's wool gently, and soon, the farm had a warm, cozy blanket. Annie felt lighter and cooler— perfect for a summer day!

Color Annie and her fluffy alpaca friends!

B - Benny the Brave Bull

Benny the Bull was big and strong but also very kind. One windy day, the barn doors slammed shut, trapping all the animals inside! "I'll help!" Benny said. He lowered his head and gently pushed the doors open with his strong horns. **"Hooray for Benny!"** cheered the animals. Benny wasn't just strong—he was a hero!

Color Benny, the brave and kind bull!

C - Clucky the Curious Chicken

Clucky loved exploring the farm. One day, she found a shiny key near the haystack. **"What could this open?"** she wondered.
She showed it to Farmer Joe, who laughed. **"Clucky, you found the key to the tool shed!"** Thanks to her curiosity, Farmer Joe could fix the fence.

Color Clucky, the curious chicken!

D - Dilly the Dancing Duck

Dilly the Duck loved to dance! Every morning, she waddled to the pond, flapped her wings, and spun in circles.
One day, the farm animals gathered to watch her. **"Go, Dilly!"** cheered the chickens. Even the cows mooed along to her happy splashes.
Farmer Joe smiled.
"Dilly, you've got the best moves on the farm!"
Dilly quacked with joy and kept on dancing!

Color Dilly, the dancing duck!

E - Ellie the Energetic Emu

Ellie loved to run fast! One day, Farmer Joe needed help delivering apples. **"Ellie, can you take these to the farmhouse?"** he asked. Ellie zoomed off and delivered them in no time. **"Hooray for Ellie!"** cheered the animals.

Color Ellie, the speedy emu!

F - Freddie the Friendly Frog

Freddie the Frog loved to hop around the farm's pond. One rainy day, the little ducklings couldn't find their way home. **"Follow me!"** croaked Freddie as he hopped from lily pad to lily pad. The ducklings followed him safely back to their nest. **"Hooray for Freddie!"** quacked their mother.

Color Freddie, thefriendly frog!

8

G - Gus the Gentle Goat

Gus the Goat loved to nibble on grass and explore the farm. One day, he found a little lamb stuck behind the fence.
"I'll help!" said Gus. He gently nudged the fence until the lamb wiggled free.
"Thank you, Gus!" bleated the lamb.

Color Gus, the gentle goat!

9

H - Holly the Happy Horse

Holly the Horse loved galloping across the fields. One afternoon, Farmer Joe's hat blew away in the wind! **"I'll get it!"** neighed Holly as she raced after it. She caught the hat just in time. **"Great job, Holly!"** said Farmer Joe.

Color Holly, the happy horse!

I - Izzy the Imaginative Iguana

Izzy the Iguana loved to climb and explore the farm. She imagined she was a pirate sailing the high seas on the barn roof!

One day, she spotted a missing basket of apples. **"Aha! A treasure!"** she said. She showed Farmer Joe, who laughed.

"Great job, Izzy!" he said. **"You're the best explorer on the farm!"**

Color Izzy, the imaginative iguana!

J - Jack the Joyful Jackrabbit

Jack the Jackrabbit loved to jump! Every morning, he bounced all over the farm, making the animals laugh.
One day, a little chick got stuck on the wrong side of the fence. **"I'll help!"** said Jack. With one big hop, he landed beside the chick and guided it home. **"Hooray for Jack!"** cheered the animals.

Color Jack,the joyful jackrabbit!

12

K - Katie the Kind Kitten

Katie the Kitten loved to cuddle. One chilly morning, she found a shivering puppy by the barn. **"Come here, little friend!"** purred Katie as she curled up beside him. The puppy warmed up and wagged his tail happily. **"Katie, you're so kind!"** said Farmer Joe.

Color Katie, the kind kitten!

L - Lily the Laughing Llama

Lily the Llama loved to giggle! She laughed at the bouncing bunnies, the waddling ducks, and even at her own fluffy reflection in the pond.
One day, a grumpy goat was feeling down. Lily told him a funny joke, and soon, he was laughing too!
"Laughter makes everything better!" said Lily.

Color Lily, the laughing llama!

14

M - Milo the Mischievous Mouse

Milo the Mouse loved to play hide and seek! He scurried around the barn, hiding in hay piles and behind buckets. One day, he found Farmer Joe's lost watch under a sack of grain. **"Look whatI found!"** squeaked Milo. **"Great job, Milo!"** said Farmer Joe. **"You're a tiny hero!"**

Color Milo, the mischievous mouse!

N - Nanny
the Nice Newt

Nanny the Newt was the smallest animal on the farm, but she had the biggest heart! She loved helping others. One day, she saw a butterfly stuck in a spider's web. Carefully, she freed it with her tiny tail. **"Thank you, Nanny!"** fluttered the butterfly. **"You're so kind!"**

Color Nanny, the nice newt!

O - Ollie the Observant Owl

Ollie the Owl loved watching over the farm from his tree. He saw everything—day and night!
One evening, he spotted a little lamb wandering too far.
"Baa! I'm lost!" cried the lamb.
"Follow my hoots!" called Ollie. With his help, the lamb found its way home.

Color Ollie, the observant owl!

P - Penny the Playful Pig

Penny the Pig loved to splash in the mud! She rolled and giggled, making funny snorting sounds. One day, she saw a sad duck who had lost his toy. Penny searched the mud and found it! **"Quack! Thank you, Penny!"** said the duck.

Color Penny, the playful pig!

18

Q - Quinn the Quick Quail

Quinn the Quail loved to run! He dashed around the farm, zigzagging between the animals.One day, a strong wind blew Farmer Joe's hat away. **"I'll get it!"** chirped Quinn. He raced after the hat and caught it just in time. **"Great job, Quinn!"** cheered the animals.

Color Quinn, the quick

R - Rocky the Reliable Rooster

Rocky the Rooster woke up early every morning to crow and wake up the farm. **"Cock-a-doodle-doo!"** he called.
One day, a sleepy cow almost missed breakfast! **"Thanks for waking me up, Rocky!"** she mooed.
"That's my job!" Rocky said proudly.

Color Rocky, the reliable rooster!

S - Sally the Soft Sheep

Sally the Sheep had the fluffiest wool on the farm. She loved playing with her friends in the meadow. One chilly evening, a little rabbit was shivering. **"Come snuggle with me!"** said Sally. The rabbit curled up in her soft wool and felt warm again.

Color Sally, the soft sheep!

T - Tommy the Talkative Turkey

Tommy the Turkey loved to gobble all day long. **"Gobble, gobble!"** he called to everyone on the farm.
One day, Farmer Joe couldn't find his missing glove. Tommy called out, **"Look by the haystack!"** Sure enough, the glove was there! **"Great job, Tommy!"** said Farmer Joe.

Color Tommy, the talkative turkey!

U - Umi the Unique Unicorn

Umi the Unicorn was special—she had a shimmering mane and loved to spread joy on the farm.
One rainy day, the animals felt gloomy. Umi twirled and **poof!** A rainbow appeared in the sky!
"Wow! You made the day magical, Umi!" cheered the animals.

**Color Umi,
the unique unicorn!**

V - Victor the Very Helpful Vulture

Victor the Vulture loved soaring high above the farm, watching everything below.
One day, a little goat got stuck behind a fallen fence. **"Baa! Help!"** he cried.
Victor quickly flew to Farmer Joe. **"Come fast! The goat needs you!"** Farmer Joe fixed the fence, and the goat was safe. **"Thank you, Victor!"** cheered the animals.

Color Victor, the very helpful vulture!

W - Wally the Wiggly Worm

Wally the Worm loved to wiggle through the soil, helping the plants grow big and strong. One day, a tiny seed was stuck under a rock. Wally wiggled and pushed until the seed was free! Soon, a beautiful flower grew. **"Thank you, Wally!"** said the farm animals. Color Wally, the wiggly

Color Wally, the wiggly worm!

X - Xavier the Excited Xerus

Xavier the Xerus loved to scamper around the farm, collecting nuts and seeds.
One day, the wind blew his pile of acorns away! **"Oh no!"** he squeaked. The farm animals helped him gather the acorns again. **"Thank you, friends!"** Xavier cheered.

Color Xavier, the excited xerus!

Y - Yara the Yawning Yak

Yara the Yak loved napping in the soft grass. She yawned so big that even the chickens started yawning! One day, a little lamb couldn't sleep. **"Try a big yawn like me!"** said Yara. The lamb yawned, snuggled up, and soon fell asleep.

Color Yara, the yawning yak!

Z - Zane the Zippy Zebra

Zane the Zebra loved to run across the farm, his black-and-white stripes shining in the sun. One day, a baby chick couldn't keep up with her family. **"Hop on my back!"** said Zane. He trotted happily and brought her home safely.

Color Zane, the zippy zebra!

A to Z Farm Animals List

A - Alpaca

B - Bull

C - Chicken

D - Duck

E - Emu

F - Frog

G - Goat

H - Horse

I - Indian Runner Duck

J - Jackrabbit

K - Kitten (Farm Cat)

L - Llama

M - Mule

N - Newt

O - Ox

P - Pig

Q - Quail

R - Rooster

S - Sheep

T - Turkey

U - Upland Goose

V - Vulture (Some farms have them around)

W - Worm (Great for farm soil)

X - Xerus (A type of ground squirrel)

Y - Yak

Z - Zebra (Found in some exotic farms)

A-Z Uppercase and Lowercase

A a B b C c D d E e F f G g H h I l J j K k L l M m

N n O o P p Q q R r S s T t U u V v W w X x Y y Z z

Children Activity Area

Write Something About Your Favorite Animal

_____

_____

_____

_____

_____

Write Something If You Had A Pet Elephant

If I Were an Animal for a Day

_____

_____

_____

_____

_____

_____

My Animal Adventure Story

_____

_____

_____

_____

_____

_____

_____

Zoo or Jungle? Where Would You Go and Why?

_____

_____

_____

_____

_____

_____

_____

How will you Take Care of your Animal

_____

_____

_____

_____

_____

_____

How you will Build your Animal House

_____

_____

_____

_____

_____

_____

_____

What will you do If you Have Animal Powers

_____

_____

_____

_____

_____

_____

_____

" Our All Animal Friends are Mixed up. Can you Unscramble their names? You're a Farm animal expert, Let's Fix them Together "

- **LACPAA**   __ __ __ __ __ __
- **ULBL**   __ __ __ __
- **IHCEKCN**   __ __ __ __ __ __ __
- **UCDK**   __ __ __ __
- **UEM**   __ __ __
- **GORF**   __ __ __ __
- **AOGT**   __ __ __ __
- **SEROH**   __ __ __ __ __
- **IUNAGA**   __ __ __ __ __ __
- **IBBTRA**   __ __ __ __ __ __
- **TTENKI**   __ __ __ __ __ __
- **LALAM**   __ __ __ __ __

- **ESOMU**   __ __ __ __ __

- **WETN**   __ __ __ __

- **LWO**   __ __ __

- **GPI**   __ __ __

- **LAIUQ**   __ __ __ __ __

- **STOORE**   __ __ __ __ __ __

- **HESEP**   __ __ __ __ __

- **TRUYEK**   __ __ __ __ __ __

- **RNCONUI**   __ __ __ __ __ __ __

- **VLUETUR**   __ __ __ __ __ __ __

- **MOWR**   __ __ __ __

- **EXSRU**   __ __ __ __ __

- **KYA**   __ __ __

- **RAZBE**   __ __ __ __ __

About the Author

Yemi Oluwoye is a devoted mother and educational assistant who finds inspiration in teaching her children and the many curious young minds she works with. She creates joyful, meaningful stories that encourage creativity, curiosity, and confidence in every child.

www.ingramcontent.com/pod-product-compliance
Lightning Source LLC
Chambersburg PA
CBHW081003140626
46546CB00018B/3105